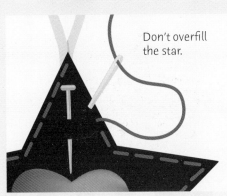

Don't overfill the star.

7. Fill the star with stuffing or cotton balls, pushing it into the points of the star. Then, pin the gap and sew the edges together. Finish off.

If you hang several stars together make the ribbons different lengths.

# Reindeer collage

Leave a small gap between each part of the body.

Use a pale material for the antlers and tummy.

1. For the background, cut a rectangle from a piece of blue material. Cut a curved strip from white material for the snow and glue it at the bottom.

2. Draw simple shapes for a reindeer's head, body, tail and legs on paper, like this. Draw a pair of antlers, too. Then, cut out each shape.

3. Pin the paper shapes onto pieces of material, then cut around them. Cut shapes from material for the nose and tummy, too.

4. Arrange all the pieces of material for the reindeer's body on the background. Then, glue on each piece with a little white glue.

5. Cut two leaf shapes and a triangle for the trees. Then, cut out circles from the white material for snowflakes. Glue them onto the background.

# Christmas things to stitch and sew

Fiona Watt

Designed and illustrated by Katrina Fearn

Additional design and illustration by Nelupa Hussain

Steps illustrated by Jo Moore
Photographs by Howard Allman

## Contents

# Hanging stars

1. Draw the outline of a star on a piece of thin paper and cut it out. Fold a piece of material in half and pin the star onto it.

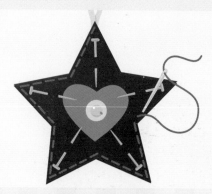

Use the ideas shown here for decorating stars with different shapes.

2. Carefully cut around the star through both layers of material. Then, remove the pins and put one of the stars to one side.

Glue the heart below one of the points of the star, like this.

3. Cut a small heart from another piece of material. Put a few dots of white glue on the back of the heart and press it in the middle of the star.

4. Thread a needle and bring it up from the back, in the middle of the heart. Follow the steps on page 32 for stitching on a sequin and a bead.

5. To make a loop for hanging, cut a piece of thin ribbon. Then, glue the ends onto one of the points of the undecorated star.

6. Pin the stars together, with the loop at the top. Then, sew around the edges with little running stitches (see page 30) but leave a gap for stuffing.

6. Thread a needle with white or cream thread. Sew several cross stitches (see page 30) on the reindeer's back. Make them different sizes.

7. Use a pencil to mark the reindeer's eyes. Then, thread a needle with brown thread and stitch a French knot over each mark (see page 30).

8. Sew a long brown stitch down each tree shape as a trunk. Sew shorter stitches for branches coming from the trunk, too.

# Tree cards

Glue the strips on at different angles.

1. Cut a rectangle of thick paper or thin cardboard and fold it in half. Glue a strip of material at an angle along the top of the card.

2. Cut another strip from a different piece of material. Glue it along the bottom of the card and trim around its edges, too.

3. Cut a tall triangle from material, for a tree. Then, cut a short strip for a trunk. Glue the trunk onto the front of the triangle, like this.

4. Thread a needle and sew a line of running stitches above the trunk. Then, spread some glue on the back of the tree and press it onto the card.

# Snowmen and penguins

Pin the paper shape through both layers of material.

Find out how to sew on a button on page 32.

1. Draw the outline of a snowman on a piece of thin paper and cut it out. Fold a piece of white material in half and pin on the snowman.

2. Cut carefully around the snowman, then remove the pins. Cut a nose from a scrap of material and glue it onto one of the snowman pieces.

3. Thread a needle and sew a French knot (see page 30) for each eye. Then, sew two buttons in a line on the snowman's tummy.

4. Pin the two body pieces together. Then, sew them together with running stitches. Leave a gap at one side of the body for stuffing.

Cut a rounded shape for a penguin's body, then add the tummy, beak, flippers and feet (see the page opposite).

Penguin

5. Fill the snowman's head and body with stuffing or cotton balls. Then, pin the edges of the body again and sew the shapes together. Finish off.

6. Cut a strip of material for a scarf, making sure that it fits around the snowman's neck. Then, wrap it around the neck and tie a knot.

To make a penguin, cut out wings and flippers and glue them onto the wrong side of one body shape before you sew the pieces together.

# Holly wreath

1. For the back of the wreath, draw around a saucer on a piece of thick paper. Then, put a mug in the middle of the circle and draw around it, too.

Snip the bend in the middle of the circle.

2. Cut out the big circle. Then, bend the circle in half and snip the bend. Poke the tip of your scissors through the hole and cut out the middle circle.

This will give you two leaves.

3. Draw a holly leaf on a piece of thin paper and cut it out. Then, fold a piece of material in half. Pin the shape onto the material and cut around it.

4. Cut out lots more leaves from different shades and patterns of green material. You'll need to cut out about 20 leaves altogether.

5. Cut out circles from different pieces of material, for decorations. Then, add cross stitches and stars (see steps 3 and 4 on page 24).

You could tie a bow in some ribbon and sew it onto a wreath.

6. Glue the leaves all over the paper ring, overlapping some of them. Then, glue the circles on top. Tape a ribbon on the back for hanging.

# Christmas stockings

Cut through both layers of material.

1. Draw a stocking on a piece of thin paper and cut it out. Fold a piece of material in half and pin the stocking to it. Then, cut around the shape.

2. Unpin the shapes. Then, cut a strip of material and glue it along the top of one of the stocking pieces. Trim the ends of the strip.

3. Cut out shapes from different materials and glue them on, too. Then, sew stars onto the stocking, following steps 3 and 4 on page 24.

Use the ideas shown here for different ways of decorating a stocking.

4. If you want to add a loop for hanging, cut a piece of ribbon and fold it in half. Glue the ends to one side of the undecorated stocking.

5. Pin the two stocking shapes together. Then, thread a needle and sew along one side of the stocking with little running stitches.

6. Sew around the toe and along the other side, but don't sew along the top of the stocking so that you can fill it with little things. Finish off.

You could make a stocking and use it as a gift bag.

13

# Gift tags

You could sew beads onto the leaves, like those on the tag below.

## Collage tag

1. Put a cup or small mug on a piece of thick paper and draw around it. Draw around a small jar lid on another piece of paper. Cut out the circles.

2. Lay the smaller circle on top of the large one. Hold them together, like this, then make a hole through both shapes with a hole puncher.

3. Cut out two holly leaves from a piece of material. Thread a needle and sew a line of running stitches along the middle of each one.

4. Then, snip a little hole in the end of each leaf. Cut a piece of thin ribbon and thread it through the circles and the leaves, then tie a knot.

# Simple star tag

If you don't have a luggage tag, make one from thick paper.

1. Draw a star on some paper and cut it out. Pin it onto a piece of material and cut around it. Then, glue the star onto a luggage label.

2. Thread a needle and push it up from the back of the tag, at the edge of the star. Then, do short straight stitches over the sides of the star.

3. Then, lay a button in the middle of the star and sew it on, following the steps on page 32. Finish off neatly on the back of the tag.

You could decorate a luggage tag with mistletoe or a tree, instead of a star.

# Dangling Santa

Sew a ribbon on the top of the tree or Santa for hanging.

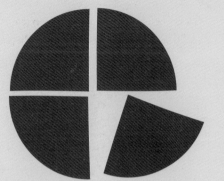

1. Lay a large plate on a piece of red material and draw around it. Cut out the circle you have drawn. Then, cut the circle into quarters.

2. Cut a shape for the hair and beard from white material, so that it fits on one quarter, like this. Then, glue the shape on.

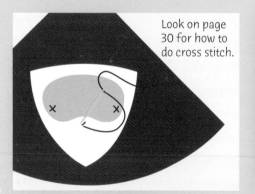

Look on page 30 for how to do cross stitch.

3. Cut out a shape for the face and glue it onto the beard. Sew a red cross stitch on each cheek. Then, sew a smaller one on the beard for a mouth.

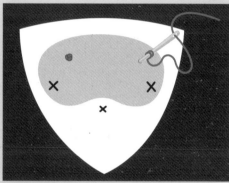

4. Mark the position of the eyes with a pencil. Then, sew a French knot (see page 30) over each mark. Try to make the stitches the same size.

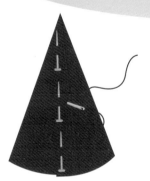

5. Fold the material to make a cone. Overlap the edges and pin them together. Sew the edges together with little running stitches.

Look on page 32 to find out how to sew on a button.

6. Cut two strips for legs. Then, cut out gloves, a circle for the top of the hat, and feet. Glue them onto the body, then sew buttons on the feet and gloves.

# Christmas tree

1. Follow step 1 on the opposite page using green material. Then, cut out several little circles from different materials for the decorations.

Sew the stitches at different angles.

2. Glue the decorations onto one of the quarters, spacing them out, like this. Then, sew lots of straight stitches in between them.

3. Cut a strip of material for the trunk and glue the top of it onto the tree. Then, follow step 5 opposite for sewing the tree together.

You could glue a star on top of the tree.

The trunk dangles down the middle of the tree.

# Sparkly decorations

Don't cut
along the fold.

Make the circles
different sizes.

1. Fold a small piece of thin paper in half and draw the shape of half a decoration against the fold, like this. Then, cut around the shape.

2. Unfold the paper and pin it onto a piece of material. Cut around the shape. Then, cut two circles from other pieces of material.

3. Glue the circles onto the decoration. Then, cut a little star from another piece of material. Glue it onto the decoration, like this.

4. Thread a needle with some thread, then sew on a sequin and a little bead in the middle of the star, following the steps on page 32.

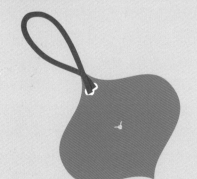

5. To make a loop for hanging, cut a piece of thin ribbon and fold it in half. Spread glue on the ends of the ribbon and press them onto the back.

# Pretty gift bags

1. Cut a long rectangle from a piece of material and fold it in half. Push two pins into the material to mark the fold, then unfold it.

2. Turn the material over so that the wrong side of it is showing. Then, fold over about 2cm (¾in) at one end and pin it.

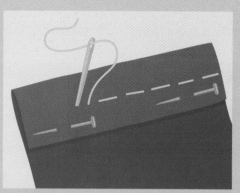

3. Sew a line of running stitches to secure the folded material, like this. Then, fold over the other end and sew it in the same way.

4. Then, cut a piece of net or wide ribbon. Tie two pieces of thick thread around the middle. Don't cut off the trailing ends of the thread.

To close the gift bags, pull both ribbons at the same time.

Sew French knots (see page 30) around the ribbon decoration.

Stop sewing when you reach the folded edge.

5. Fold a short ribbon in half. Lay it on the material and put the net on top. Then, sew on a button, securing the net and the ribbon at the same time.

6. Then, fold the material in half again with the right sides together. Pin the edges, then sew along each one with little running stitches.

Use a blunt needle with a large eye.

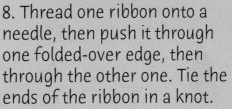

7. Turn the bag inside out. Then, cut two pieces of ribbon or cord which are about three times the width of the bag.

8. Thread one ribbon onto a needle, then push it through one folded-over edge, then through the other one. Tie the ends of the ribbon in a knot.

9. Starting at the opposite side of the bag to the first ribbon, push the other ribbon through the folded-over edges. Then, tie the ends in a knot, again.

# Angels

Cut through both layers of material.

Bring the needle up from the back at the edge of the face.

1. Draw a shape for an angel's body on thin paper and cut it out. Fold a piece of material in half, pin the shape onto it, and then cut around it.

2. Cut a round shape for the face from a small piece of plain material. Pin it at the top of one of the body pieces, a little way in from the edge.

3. Bring your needle up from the back and do a little stitch onto the face. Then, bring the needle up again a little way away and do another stitch.

4. Stitch all the way around the face, then mark the position of the eyes with a pencil. Sew a French knot (see page 30) for each eye.

5. Sew two little lines for the mouth with red thread. Cut out two hands from the same material as the face and glue them on.

Glue the wings onto the right side of the material.

6. For the wings, fold a piece of material in half and cut out a wing shape through both layers. Glue them like this, onto the other body shape.

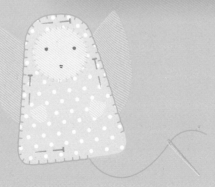

7. Then, pin the two body shapes together, like this. Use blanket stitch (see page 31) to sew around the edge, but leave a gap for stuffing.

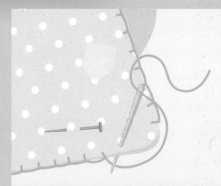

8. Fill the angel with stuffing or cotton balls, but don't overfill it. Pin the edges of the gap, then stitch them together to finish the angel.

# Snowflake chains

1. Put a small jar lid on a piece of paper, draw around it, then cut it out. Pin the circle on a piece of material and cut around it.

2. Cut out five more circles in the same way. Then, glue the circles onto a darker piece of material. Cut around each circle leaving a small border.

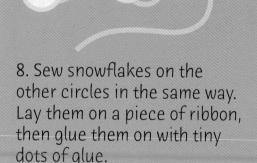

3. Thread a needle with a long piece of white thread, then sew a cross stitch in the middle of each circle (see page 30).

4. Sew another stitch across the middle of the cross stitch. Then, sew another one from the top to the bottom to make a 'star'.

5. Sew a straight stitch at the end of each point of the star. You don't need to finish off after each stitch just carry the thread across the back.

6. Then, sew two little stitches at an angle to make a 'V' shape at each end of each line of stitches, like this. Make them as neat as you can.

7. To complete the snowflake, sew a French knot (see page 30) between each line of stitches. Space them evenly between the lines.

8. Sew snowflakes on the other circles in the same way. Lay them on a piece of ribbon, then glue them on with tiny dots of glue.

# Christmas dove

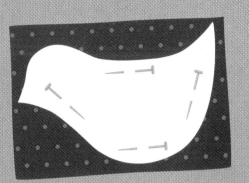

1. Draw the shape for a dove's body on a piece of thin paper and cut it out. Pin the shape onto a piece of material and cut around it.

2. Unpin the paper shape and draw a beak and a tummy on it. Cut them out. Then, pin the shapes onto other pieces of material and cut around them.

3. Glue the shapes for the tummy and the beak onto the dove. Then, cut out a simple wing and tail, like the shapes shown above.

These holly leaves were glued onto the background, then the beads and lines of stitches were added.

4. Cut curved strips of material and glue them onto the wing and the tail. Then, cut curved shapes at the ends of them and trim the edges, like this.

5. Glue the end of the body onto the tail, then glue on the wing. Cut out two feet and glue one on top and one underneath the tummy.

26

You could sew
little stars around
your dove.

Find out on page
30 how to do
the stitches.

6. Glue the dove onto a piece
of material. Then, sew a line
of running stitches along the
tummy, wing and tail. Add a
French knot for an eye, too.

7. Cut out a curved shape for
some mistletoe leaves and glue
it beside the dove. Sew a line
of running stitches for a stalk
and add lines along the leaves.

8. Sew two small beads at the
top of the mistletoe for berries.
Then, follow steps 3 to 7 on
page 24 to sew a snowflake
beside the dove.

# Present cards

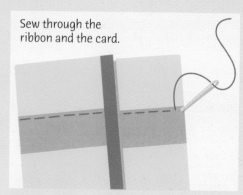
Sew through the ribbon and the card.

1. Cut a long thin rectangle for the card. Make a flap by folding the left-hand end in to just past the middle. Then, fold the other end over to meet it.

2. Glue two pieces of ribbon on the flaps, making sure that they line up. Then, glue another piece of ribbon down the edge of a flap, like this.

3. Thread a needle and sew a line of little running stitches (see page 30) along one of the ribbons. Finish off, then sew along the other ribbon.

This red card was made from a square of paper, instead of a rectangle.

4. Cut out four stars from thick paper and sew one of them near the edge of the flap. Then, sew on another star a little way below it.

5. Stitch on the other two stars in the same way, doing the stitches at different angles each time. Finish off on the back on the flap.

You could tie a little bow and sew it onto a card.

# How to do the stitches

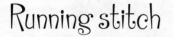
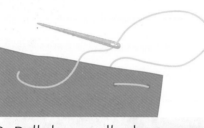

## Running stitch

Make sure you have a knot in the end of your thread.

1. Push the needle up from the back of the material and pull the thread through. Then, push the needle into the material a little way away.

2. Pull the needle down behind the material until the thread is tight. This makes a straight stitch on the front of the material.

Keep on stitching in this way to make a line of stitches.

3. Push the needle up from the back again, a little way away from the first stitch. Then, push it down again to make another stitch.

## Cross stitch

Always tie a knot at the end of your thread, first.

1. Push the needle up from the back of the material and pull the thread. Then, push the needle into the material at a diagonal, like this.

2. Pull the thread all the way through to make a diagonal stitch. Then, push the needle up from the back again beside first stitch, like this.

3. Then, push the needle in beside the top of the first stitch to make an 'X'. Pull the needle behind the material until the thread is tight.

## French knot

1. To sew a French knot, push the needle up from the back of the material. Then, hold the thread with your thumb, like this.

The thread should be wrapped twice around the needle.

2. Put the tip of your needle under the thread, then over the top, so that the thread is wound around the needle. Wind it around once more.

Keep holding the thread as you twist the needle.

3. Twist the needle around and push it back into the material near where it came out. Then, pull the thread gently to make a neat knot.

To sew a spiral like the one in the middle of this star, weave a thread in and out of running stitches.

# Blanket stitch

The knot is between the layers.

1. Lay two pieces of material with their edges together. Bring your needle up through the top layer of material, close to the edge.

2. Then, push the needle down through both layers of material, a little way away from the edge. Don't pull it all the way through yet.

# Finishing off

Continue sewing along the edge like this.

Finishing off secures the thread.

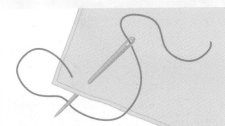

3. Put the thread under the needle, then pull the needle down gently. Keep pulling on the needle until the thread is tight and makes a stitch.

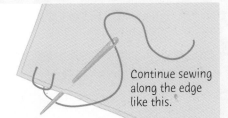

4. Push the needle into the material beside the last stitch. Then, put the thread behind the needle and pull it again to make another stitch.

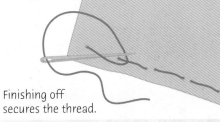

To finish sewing, push the needle through the last stitch and pull the thread. Then, stitch through the thread once more. Cut off the loose end.

# Buttons and sequins

## Sewing on a sequin

1. Push your needle up from the back of the material, but don't pull it all the way through. Slide a sequin, then a bead, onto the needle.

2. Pull the thread up through the sequin and bead. Then, push the needle back down through the hole in the sequin. Finish off.

## Sewing on a button

1. Push your needle up from the back of the material, but don't pull it all the way through. Slide one hole in a button onto the needle.

2. Pull the thread up through the hole. Then, push the needle down through the other hole. Finish off on the back of the material.

If the button has four holes, sew up through one hole, then down through the hole diagonally opposite. Do the same with the other holes.

Photographic manipulation by John Russell.
First published in 2007 by Usborne Publishing Ltd., 83-85 Saffron Hill, London, EC1N 8RT, England www.usborne.com Copyright © 2007 Usborne Publishing Ltd. The name Usborne and the devices ♀⊕ are Trade Marks of Usborne Publishing Ltd. All rights reserved. No part of this publication may be reproduced, stored in a retrieval system, or transmitted in any form or by any means, electronic, mechanical, photocopy, recording or otherwise, without prior permission of the publisher. First published in America in 2008. UE. Printed in Malaysia.